TEMPERED LEGACY

Becoming the Man Your Bloodline Prayed For

RAYMOND HENDRICKS

Men of Tempered Strength LLC
Tampa, Florida
2026

COPYRIGHT

This book is a work of personal experience, reflection, faith, and principle based guidance. It is intended for educational and inspirational purposes and is not a substitute for professional medical care, mental health treatment, counseling, legal advice, or other qualified professional services.

Published by Men of Tempered Strength LLC
Tampa, Florida, United States

ISBN: 979 8 9976728 0 5
First Men of Tempered Strength LLC Edition: 2026

Scripture references, where used, are drawn from the King James Version (KJV) or New King James Version (NKJV) unless otherwise noted.

DEDICATION

To the man reading this book,

This is for you.

For the man who knows there is more in him. For the man carrying battles no one sees, responsibilities few understand, and expectations he was never taught how to carry.

For the man determined to become stronger without becoming hardened, disciplined without losing compassion, and successful without losing himself.

Maybe no one showed you how to build a legacy. Maybe you inherited wounds, habits, and patterns you never asked for. But what was handed to you does not have to be what you hand down.

You can be the turning point.

You can be the man who breaks the cycle, raises the standard, strengthens his family, and leaves those who come after him something better than what he received.

If you are willing to do the work, confront yourself, and live with intention, these pages are for you.

May you become the man your bloodline prayed for.

And may the strength you build today become the legacy they stand on tomorrow.

Raymond Hendricks

TABLE OF CONTENTS

THE NEW STANDARD

I did not write this for you to just read it, close it, and go right back to the same life.

I wrote this book to make you look at your thinking, your choices, your leadership, and the life you are building while you still have time to shape it.

You are not here by accident. Something in you is ready to stop repeating cycles and start building systems. Something in you knows there is more to your name than what is in your bank account or on your social media page. Something in you is craving legacy over likes.

What I had to learn was simple.

There is no legacy without discipline.

There is no greatness without intentionality.

And there is no lasting change without uncomfortable conversations, especially the ones you need to have with yourself.

This book will ask you to confront habits, question motives, strengthen your relationships, build a personal code, and think about what your life is teaching the people around you.

It is not about pretending to be perfect. It is about becoming responsible for what moves through you and what moves forward because of you.

The world can set whatever standard it wants for a man.

You still have to decide what standard you are willing to live by when nobody is watching.

AUTHOR'S NOTE

There is a moment every man reaches when he realizes this life is not only about surviving. It is about building something that will still speak after he is gone.

I have written about discipline, emotional control, and the war inside the mind. Tempered Legacy turns the question outward. Once a man begins leading himself, what does he build with that leadership?

What kind of father does he become? What kind of partner, brother, leader, friend, and example does he become? What does he stop passing down? What does he begin on purpose?

Legacy is built in quiet decisions nobody applauds. It is built in how you treat people when you are frustrated. In whether your children experience your presence. In whether your word means something. In whether you can apologize, repair, rest, pray, and keep growing.

I did not write this for a perfect man. I wrote it for the man who is willing to become more intentional.

I did not write this to make you feel good for a few minutes. I wrote it because I want you to build something that can stand when life gets hard.

Let us get to work.

Raymond Hendricks

A MAP OF THE TEMPERED JOURNEY

Every man who picks up this book is somewhere along the Tempered journey.

TEMPERED MIND is about the inner battlefield. It asks what happens in your thoughts before those thoughts become reactions, habits, and consequences.

TEMPERED STRENGTH is about disciplined action. It asks whether you can govern emotion, structure your days, and build habits strong enough to carry pressure.

TEMPERED LEGACY is about what moves forward. It asks what your discipline becomes in the lives of other people. It is about family, leadership, fatherhood, brotherhood, values, systems, traditions, healing, and the kind of name you leave behind.

Mind. Strength. Legacy.

Think clearly.

Live with discipline.

Build what outlives you.

You are building your legacy whether you think about it or not. My goal is to help you build it on purpose.

CHAPTER 1

COMMANDING THE INNER COURT

Lead yourself before you lead anything else.

The First Kingdom

Every man has a kingdom, even if nobody calls it that. Before there is a business, a household, a platform, a title, or a bank account, there is the territory inside you. Your thoughts live there. Your moods live there. Your fears, habits, memories, pride, discipline, and convictions live there too. That inner territory is the first place a man learns to lead, and it is the first place a man learns to lose control.

A lot of men want authority outside themselves before they have order inside themselves. We want people to respect our decisions while we are still being ruled by impulses. We want peace in the house while we carry chaos into every room. We want our children to listen while we have not learned to listen to our own conscience. We want trust without consistency.

That is the reason I call this the Inner Court. It is the room nobody sees, but everybody around you feels. When the Inner Court is calm, clear, and governed, your presence changes. You do not need to announce your discipline. People can feel it. When the Inner Court is confused, bitter, reactive, or exhausted, that shows up too. It shows up in your tone. In your decisions. In what you tolerate. In what you avoid. In how quickly you become defensive.

Legacy starts here. It starts with what you allow to lead you today, long before anybody reads your will or talks about what you left behind.

Who Is Sitting on the Throne?

Ask yourself a hard question: who takes control of you when pressure arrives?

Is it the disciplined man you say you are becoming, or is it the wounded version of you that learned to survive years ago? Is it wisdom, or ego? Is it patience, or fear? Is it purpose, or the need to prove something?

Most of us have more than one voice inside. There is the part of us that knows better, and there is the part that wants relief right now. There is the man who wants to protect his future, and there is the boy who still wants to fight every battle from the past. Maturity is not pretending those voices do not exist. Maturity is deciding which one gets authority.

You can be angry without giving anger the throne. You can be hurt without allowing hurt to write policy for your life. You can be disappointed without letting disappointment turn into destruction. You can be afraid and still move with courage.

Self government is not emotional numbness. It is emotional leadership. The goal is not to stop feeling. The goal is to stop handing every feeling a set of keys.

The Cost of an Ungoverned Life

An ungoverned man pays for his lack of discipline in places he never expected.

He may pay for it in relationships because every disagreement becomes a battle. He may pay for it financially because impulse gets mistaken for freedom. He may pay for it professionally because pride makes correction feel like disrespect. He may pay for it spiritually because he stays too distracted to hear what his life is trying to teach him.

The hardest part is that the bill often comes later. One angry sentence can take ten seconds to say and ten years to repair. One dishonest decision can destroy a reputation that took years to build. One pattern of emotional absence can become the childhood your children spend adulthood trying to understand.

That is the reason discipline has to be built before the crisis comes. You need the brakes before the accident, not after it.

A tempered man trains himself while things are calm. He practices the pause. He becomes familiar with his triggers. He notices when he is tired, embarrassed, rejected, or insecure. He develops a way to return to center before he needs it most.

Presence Before Power

Some men think leadership is about being the strongest voice in the room. I have learned that leadership often looks quieter than that.

Sometimes it is the ability to remain present while another person is emotional. Sometimes it is admitting, "I was wrong." Sometimes it is saying, "I need a minute before I answer." Sometimes it is leaving an argument without abandoning the relationship.

When you stay present, you still have choices. Once you react without thinking, you usually give those choices away.

When you are present, you can ask what the moment actually requires. Does it require correction? Does it require silence? Does it require an apology? Does it require a boundary? Does it require rest? Does it require a conversation that you have been avoiding?

The man who commands his Inner Court does not ask only, "What do I feel like doing?" He asks, "What kind of man does this moment require me to be?"

That question is one of the foundations of legacy. Your family will remember how you handled pressure more than they remember the speeches you gave about strength.

Build a Morning Government

If you want more command over your life, stop beginning every day by handing your attention to everybody else.

Before the phone, before the messages, before the noise, take a few minutes to govern yourself. You do not need a complicated routine. You need a consistent one.

Ask yourself four questions: What am I thinking? What am I feeling? What matters most today? What would the disciplined version of me do first?

Then make one decision before the world starts making decisions for you. Maybe you pray. Maybe you journal. Maybe you stretch, walk, read, or sit quietly. The specific practice matters less than the principle. Start the day from your center.

Over time, this changes the way you move. You become less available to chaos because you have already decided who you are before chaos calls your name.

The real crown is not worn. It is earned in the private moments when you govern yourself without applause.

LEGACY WORK 1

Do not rush this page. Write what is true.

1. What emotion most often takes the throne when I am under pressure?

2. What has that reaction cost me?

3. What does self government look like in one specific situation this week?

4. Who experiences the best and worst of my inner life?

5. What morning practice will help me return to center?

THIS WEEK'S ACTION

Choose one daily practice and keep it for seven days before adding anything else.

NOTES

CHAPTER 2

PURPOSE IN PRECISION

The clearer your aim, the stronger your impact.

Purpose Is Not a Mood

Most men want purpose. Very few men are willing to get precise about it. We like the idea of being called to something, but purpose gets uncomfortable when it requires us to choose. Precision means some good opportunities will still be wrong for you. It means some relationships will not fit the man you are becoming. It means your calendar cannot say yes to everything and still claim that your mission matters.

Purpose is not a mood you wake up with. It is a direction you keep returning to.

You can feel inspired one day and confused the next. That does not mean your purpose disappeared. It means feelings changed. A clear man knows the difference between his assignment and his emotional weather.

When purpose is vague, everything looks important. Every invitation feels urgent. Every distraction gets a vote. But when purpose becomes specific, you gain a filter. You can ask, "Does this strengthen what I am building, or does it pull me away from it?"

That question will save you time, money, energy, and years.

Scattered Power

Unclear purpose produces scattered power. You can be busy from sunrise to midnight and still build nothing that lasts. Activity can make you feel productive because it gives you movement, but movement and progress are not the same thing.

Think about a man trying to dig ten wells one foot deep. He works hard. He sweats. He uses energy. But he never reaches water. Another man chooses one place and keeps digging. From the outside, his work may look slower. In reality, he is going deeper.

Legacy requires depth.

There are seasons when you have to stop asking what else you can add and start asking what needs to be removed. What obligation has become a distraction? What habit keeps stealing your best hours? What relationship consistently pulls you away from your values? What project are you maintaining only because your ego does not want to let it go?

Precision is not only choosing what matters. It is having the courage to release what no longer does.

Write the Mission in Plain Language

Your purpose should be clear enough that you can explain it without performing.

Try this sentence: I exist to _______ so that _______. I commit to _______ no matter the season.

Do not try to make it sound impressive. Make it true.

For me, the language of legacy has always come back to helping people become stronger, more disciplined, more emotionally aware, and more intentional about what they pass forward. The words may evolve as life evolves, but the center stays recognizable.

Your statement might focus on fatherhood, business, ministry, art, service, education, community, or simply becoming the first stable man in your family line. Purpose does not have to be famous to be powerful.

A man who faithfully changes the emotional climate of one household may impact more lives than a man with a million followers and no peace at home.

The Difference Between Opportunity and Assignment

One of the hardest lessons for an ambitious man is that every open door is not his door.

Some opportunities feed ego but starve purpose. Some pay well but cost too much internally. Some look like elevation but pull you away from the people and values you said mattered most. Wisdom is being able to recognize the difference.

Before you say yes, ask three things. Does this align with my values? Does this move my mission forward? What will this yes require me to say no to?

Every yes spends something. Time. Attention. Energy. Presence. Money. Focus. Sometimes sleep. Sometimes peace.

Precision means you count the cost before you commit.

A man of legacy does not build by collecting everything. He builds by arranging the right things in the right order.

Aim With Legacy in Mind

Think of purpose like an arrow. Strength alone will not make it land where it needs to land. You can pull the string hard, but without aim the arrow only travels fast in the wrong direction.

Your form matters. Your focus matters. Your target matters.

Ask yourself who benefits if you live your purpose well. Your children? Your future employees? Your neighborhood? Your church? Men you may never meet? The people whose lives will be different because you refused to waste your gifts?

Then ask the harder question: what happens if you refuse to become precise?

There is a cost to unused purpose. There is a cost to endless distraction. There is a cost to constantly restarting because you never committed long enough to build momentum.

Purpose without precision becomes potential without power. Choose your aim. Then keep your life pointed toward it.

LEGACY WORK 2

Do not rush this page. Write what is true.

1. What am I building that should outlast me?

____

____

____

____

____

____

2. What three activities consume time without strengthening that mission?

____

____

____

____

____

____

3. What values will I refuse to compromise?

____

____

____

____

____

____

4. What opportunity do I need to say no to?

____

____

____

____

____

____

5. Write your purpose statement in one clear sentence.

____

____

THIS WEEK'S ACTION

Remove one distraction from your calendar and replace it with one action tied directly to your mission.

NOTES

CHAPTER 3

THE INHERITANCE OF SILENCE

What was never spoken can still shape a generation.

What Men Inherit

Every man inherits something. Some inherit property. Some inherit money. Some inherit debt. Many of us inherit patterns that never had a name.

For a lot of men, especially Black men, one of those inheritances is silence. Not only the silence of fathers who were absent, but sometimes the silence of fathers who were right there. Men who worked, provided, protected, and handled responsibilities, but never learned how to talk about fear, grief, tenderness, shame, or disappointment.

A child can live in the same house with a man and still know very little about his inner life.

That silence teaches without speaking. It can teach a boy that strength means never needing anyone. That crying is dangerous. That affection is optional. That pain should be swallowed. That love is proven only through provision.

Some of those lessons may have helped earlier generations survive. But survival strategies can become emotional prisons when they are passed down without examination.

The Things We Needed to Hear

Think about what you needed to hear as a boy.

Maybe it was, "I see you." Maybe it was, "I am proud of you." Maybe it was, "You do not have to earn my love." Maybe it was, "It is okay to be afraid." Maybe you needed a man to tell you that failure did not make you a failure.

When those words are missing, boys create explanations. Children are meaning makers. If a father is distant, a child may decide he is not worth closeness. If correction comes without affection, he may decide love always feels like pressure. If nobody talks about grief, he may decide pain is something to hide.

Those private conclusions can follow a man for decades.

He may become successful and still chase approval. He may become a father and still struggle to say "I love you." He may be surrounded by people and still feel emotionally alone.

Silence does not disappear because we get older. It changes clothes.

Breaking Silence Without Blaming

Breaking a generational pattern does not require you to hate the men who came before you. Understanding is not the same as excusing, and forgiveness is not the same as pretending harm did not happen.

Many of our fathers and grandfathers were carrying things they did not have language for. War. Racism. Poverty. Addiction. Loss. Violence. Humiliation. Their world may have rewarded toughness and punished vulnerability. Some did the best they could. Some did real damage. Sometimes both are true.

Your responsibility is not to rewrite their story. Your responsibility is to decide what continues through you.

You can honor what they survived while refusing to repeat what hurt you. You can appreciate provision and still choose more emotional presence. You can love a man and still tell the truth about what was missing.

Maturity can hold complexity.

Give Language to the House

If silence was inherited, language can become part of the healing.

Say the things that healthy men sometimes struggle to say. Tell your children you love them before they have to earn a moment of pride. Tell your brother when you are struggling. Tell your partner what is happening inside you before your distance turns into confusion. Apologize with complete sentences. Ask questions you were never allowed to ask.

A house changes when people know emotions can be named without becoming weapons.

That does not mean every conversation becomes dramatic. It means honesty becomes normal. "I am frustrated." "I am scared." "I need help." "I was wrong." "I need some time to think." "I am proud of you."

Those sentences can become generational infrastructure.

Do Not Let Silence Be Your Legacy

This week, write a letter to the man you needed when you were younger. It could be your father, an uncle, a mentor, or an imagined older version of yourself.

Write what you needed to hear. Do not edit it for toughness. Write it honestly.

Then choose one sentence from that letter and give it to somebody else. A son. A nephew. A younger man. A friend. Speak the words forward.

Legacy is not only what you build financially. It is what becomes emotionally possible because you were willing to speak.

You can be the man who ends a family tradition of silence without disrespecting where you came from. You can be the first man in your line who says what love needs to say.

Speak. Feel. Lead.

The goal is not to become louder. The goal is to become more truthful.

LEGACY WORK 3

Do not rush this page. Write what is true.

1. What did I need to hear growing up that I rarely heard?

2. What emotional pattern did I inherit from the men before me?

3. What part of that pattern deserves compassion?

4. What part must end with me?

5. Who needs to hear an honest word from me this week?

THIS WEEK'S ACTION

Speak one life giving sentence to a younger person or family member that you wish someone had spoken to you.

NOTES

CHAPTER 4

CARRYING GHOSTS IN BROAD DAYLIGHT

You do not have to be dead to be haunted.

Functioning While Fractured

Have you ever walked into a room full of people and still felt alone? Laughed while something inside you was hurting? Showed up as the protector while carrying wounds nobody ever asked about?

That is what it means to carry ghosts in broad daylight.

Ghosts are the memories that still have a voice. Rejection. Betrayal. Abandonment. Shame. The moment you were humiliated. The relationship that changed how you trust. The season when you had to become strong before you were ready.

Men become very good at functioning while fractured. We go to work. We pay bills. We handle responsibilities. We make jokes. We pray. We date. We raise children. From the outside, life keeps moving. Inside, old moments keep replaying.

A wound does not have to stop you from functioning to still be shaping you.

When the Past Starts Driving

Unprocessed pain rarely announces itself as unprocessed pain.

Sometimes it shows up as a short temper. Sometimes as jealousy. Sometimes as emotional distance. Sometimes as overworking. Sometimes as the need to control everything because uncertainty once hurt you. Sometimes as leaving first so nobody gets the chance to leave you.

The current situation may be small, but the reaction is carrying the weight of ten older situations.

That is the reason self awareness matters. When you notice a response that is much bigger than the moment, ask what else has entered the room.

Is this only about what she said, or did it touch an old wound? Is this only about your boss correcting you, or did it awaken every moment you felt disrespected? Is this only about your child making a mistake, or are you reacting from fear about how the world will treat him?

You cannot change a pattern you refuse to investigate.

Facing the Ghost Without Living With It

Healing does not mean you have to relive everything forever. It means the past loses the authority to keep making present decisions.

Some memories need to be talked through with somebody safe and qualified. Some need prayer. Some need journaling. Some require boundaries. Some require grief. Some require accepting that an apology may never come.

The point is not to become obsessed with the past. The point is to stop letting the past operate in secret.

You can look at a memory and say, "That happened. It affected me. It taught me things. But it does not own me."

That is different from pretending you are unaffected.

Denial says, "It did not matter." Healing says, "It mattered, and I am choosing what it means now.

Turn Pain Into Information

Pain can teach without becoming your identity.

Rejection may have taught you how deeply you value belonging. Abandonment may have shown you how important consistency is. Failure may have made you more humble. Betrayal may have taught you to recognize character, not just chemistry.

The lesson is useful. Carrying the wound forever is not.

Ask what the experience taught you about yourself. Then separate the lesson from the fear.

Maybe the lesson is to choose people carefully. The fear says trust nobody.

Maybe the lesson is to build financial stability. The fear says never rest.

Maybe the lesson is to communicate clearly. The fear says control every outcome.

A tempered man keeps wisdom and releases bondage.

Write the Truth Over the Ghost

Make a list of the ghosts that still speak to you. Do not make the list dramatic. Make it accurate.

The person who said you would never be enough. The failure you still feel embarrassed about. The relationship that made you question your value. The season you felt forgotten. The mistake you still punish yourself for.

Next to each one, write a truth you are willing to live by now.

"I can learn without hating myself."

"I can be loved without performing."

"I can protect myself without closing my heart."

"I can remember without returning."

"I can build something different."

Your legacy is not measured by whether you were wounded. Every man is wounded somewhere. Legacy is measured by what you do with the wound after you become aware of it.

Do not let what haunted you become what your children inherit.

LEGACY WORK 4

Do not rush this page. Write what is true.

1. What memory still changes the way I react today?

2. What belief did I form because of that experience?

3. Is that belief still true?

4. What lesson can I keep without keeping the wound in charge?

5. Who is safe enough to help me process what I cannot carry alone?

THIS WEEK'S ACTION

Write one old story and then write the healthier truth you are choosing now.

NOTES

CHAPTER 5

THE STRENGTH TO STAY

Commitment is not captivity. Learn the difference.

Staying Is Not Always Easy

We live in a culture that celebrates the new. New job. New relationship. New city. New plan. New identity. Sometimes a new beginning is exactly what life requires. There are situations that are unsafe, destructive, abusive, or simply complete, and wisdom means leaving them.

But there are also moments when leaving is not freedom. It is avoidance.

There is a difference between leaving what is harmful and abandoning what is hard.

Legacy is built by men who learn that difference.

Some seasons require you to stay at the table and have the conversation. Stay in the process long enough to become skilled. Stay committed to healing when progress feels slow. Stay present with your children when you are tired. Stay faithful to your values when a shortcut looks easier.

Commitment is not about suffering for the sake of suffering. It is about refusing to confuse discomfort with a sign that you are supposed to run.

The Exit Habit

Some men develop an exit habit.

When work gets frustrating, they start looking for another job. When intimacy gets uncomfortable, they create distance. When a goal stops being exciting, they start a new one. When accountability shows up, they disappear.

The pattern feels like independence, but often it is fear wearing confidence.

If you grew up around instability, leaving may feel safer than being left. Quitting may feel like control. Staying long enough to be known may feel dangerous.

But you cannot build deep roots while constantly digging yourself up.

Ask yourself whether you have been leaving situations because they are truly wrong, or because they are asking more maturity from you than you want to give.

Stay With the Work

Healing is one of the places where men often want quick results. We want one conversation to fix ten years. One apology to erase a pattern. One week of discipline to create a new identity.

Real change is slower and more ordinary.

It is choosing a better response repeatedly. It is going back after a bad day. It is continuing therapy, counseling, prayer, journaling, or accountability after the emotional urgency fades. It is repairing trust through consistency rather than explanation.

You do not prove change by how strongly you feel about it. You prove it by how long you live it.

That is the strength to stay. Staying with the work until the people closest to you no longer have to take your growth on faith because they can experience it.

Presence Is a Form of Protection

Your children do not only need your money. They need access to you. Your partner does not only need your loyalty. She needs communication. Your mission does not only need your ideas. It needs your consistency.

Presence is one of the most underrated forms of leadership.

It means you are mentally in the room, not just physically there. It means you put the phone down. It means you listen long enough to understand instead of preparing a defense. It means you keep promises about small things because small promises teach people whether your word is safe.

You cannot control every outcome in a family, but your presence can create stability.

Know When Staying Becomes Self Betrayal

There is one important distinction. Strength to stay does not mean remaining in abuse, danger, exploitation, or circumstances that require you to abandon your dignity and safety.

Discipline does not demand self destruction.

A mature man knows that commitment has boundaries. He seeks wise counsel. He gets professional support when needed. He does not use the language of loyalty to excuse violence, manipulation, addiction, or repeated harm with no accountability.

Sometimes leadership means staying and repairing. Sometimes leadership means leaving safely and responsibly.

The question is not, "Can I endure this?" The better question is, "What response protects life, integrity, and the future I am responsible for?"

Stay where growth is possible. Stay with your healing. Stay with your values. Stay planted in purpose.

And when something truly needs to end, leave with clarity, not chaos.

LEGACY WORK 5

Do not rush this page. Write what is true.

1. Where do I leave too quickly when things get difficult?

2. Where have I stayed too long in something harmful?

3. What commitment deserves more consistency from me?

4. What conversation have I been avoiding?

5. What does responsible staying look like this week?

THIS WEEK'S ACTION

Have one conversation you have been postponing. Choose calm, clarity, and responsibility.

NOTES

CHAPTER 6

THE COMPASS AND THE CODE

When life gets loud, return to what you know is true.

A Man Needs Direction

A man without direction becomes vulnerable to every distraction. When you do not know where you are going, anything can look like progress.

The world is full of noise. Money. Attention. Sex. status. competition. comparison. fear. Everybody has an opinion about what a man should be. If you do not have an internal compass, outside voices will keep changing your direction.

Your compass is your clarity about what matters. It does not tell you every turn in advance. It keeps you from wandering so far that you stop recognizing yourself.

A man with a compass can take a detour without losing his destination. He can change jobs without changing values. He can lose money without losing identity. He can receive criticism without becoming whatever the critic says he is.

Direction creates stability.

Build a Personal Code

A compass tells you where you are going. A code tells you how you will travel.

Your code is a set of non negotiable standards. Not slogans. Standards.

What do you do when telling the truth costs you? What do you do when nobody will know if you cheat? How do you speak when you are angry? What do you owe your children? What do you refuse to become even if becoming it would make life easier?

A code removes some decisions from the moment. If honesty is part of your code, you do not renegotiate honesty every time lying would be convenient. If presence is part of your code, you do not wait until you feel like showing up for your family.

Discipline becomes easier when the decision was made before the temptation arrived.

Five Standards Worth Writing Down

Your code should be personal, but here are five categories worth considering.

Truth. I do not lie to others or to myself.

Responsibility. I own what is mine to own without hiding behind excuses.

Protection. I protect people, peace, and principles without becoming controlling.

Consistency. My values do not disappear when I am tired, angry, lonely, or tempted.

Repair. When I cause harm, I do the work required to make things right where repair is possible.

You may choose different words. The point is to make your standards clear enough that they can guide behavior.

Return to the Code Under Pressure

A code matters most when emotions are loud.

You will not always feel like the man you want to be. There will be days when patience is low. Days when rejection stings. Days when somebody knows exactly how to press the old wound.

That is when you return to the code.

Instead of asking, "What can I get away with?" ask, "What does my code require?"

Instead of asking, "How do I win this argument?" ask, "How do I leave this moment with my integrity?"

Instead of asking, "What will make me feel better right now?" ask, "What protects the future I say I want?"

The code is not there to make you rigid. It is there to keep temporary emotion from creating permanent damage.

Let Your Name Mean Something

Your name becomes weighty when people can predict your character.

They know you keep your word. They know you show up. They know you do not become reckless when angry. They know you can be trusted with responsibility. They know you can admit when you are wrong.

That kind of reputation is built slowly and lost quickly.

Legacy is not branding. It is consistency remembered.

Write your code. Put it somewhere you can see it. Review it weekly. Let the people closest to you tell you whether your life matches it.

When storms come, return to the code. When life gets loud, return to the compass. You are not just moving through life. You are teaching everyone connected to you what your name stands for.

LEGACY WORK 6

Do not rush this page. Write what is true.

1. What five values define my personal code?

2. Which value becomes hardest to live when I am angry or tired?

3. Where has convenience replaced conviction?

4. Who can hold me accountable to my code?

5. What sentence do I want people to associate with my name?

THIS WEEK'S ACTION

Write your five point code and place it somewhere you will see it every morning.

NOTES

CHAPTER 7

WEIGHT, NOT WEAKNESS

Heavy does not mean weak.

Name the Weight

There is a difference between being weak and being weighted.

A lot of men do not feel weak. They feel heavy. Responsibility. Grief. Financial pressure. Family expectations. Regret. Fear. The pressure to remain useful even when they are exhausted.

Because many of us were never taught to name that weight, we learned to hide it. We call it stress. We call it grinding. We call it being tired. We joke about it. We work through it. We carry it until our body, temper, or relationships start speaking for us.

Weight is real even when nobody can see it.

Naming it is not surrender. Naming it is the first step in deciding how to carry it.

Why Men Explode

A man can carry emotional weight for a long time and still function. That is part of what makes it dangerous.

He keeps going, so everybody assumes he is fine. He may assume it too. Then a small problem becomes the place where months of pressure finally break through.

That is the reason the reaction looks bigger than the moment. The moment is only the final plate on a bar that was already overloaded.

This does not excuse destructive behavior. If your anger hurts people, responsibility still belongs to you. But understanding the load helps you build a different system.

You learn to unload before you explode.

You talk. You rest. You seek help. You exercise. You pray. You journal. You set boundaries. You stop treating your nervous system like a machine that owes everybody unlimited output.

Learn to Lift Correctly

In a gym, strength is not proven by grabbing the heaviest weight with no technique. That is how people get injured.

You learn form. You know your limits. You use a spotter. You rest between sessions. You build gradually.

Emotional strength works the same way.

You need form. A way to process pressure without harming yourself or other people.

You need limits. The ability to say, "I cannot take on one more thing right now."

You need spotters. Men, mentors, counselors, pastors, coaches, or trusted people who can help you see what you cannot see alone.

You need recovery. Sleep. Quiet. Play. Prayer. Time without performance.

Carrying weight well is a skill.

Vulnerability With Discernment

Not everybody deserves access to your most vulnerable places. Openness without discernment can become another kind of danger.

The answer is not isolation. The answer is wise connection.

Find people who can hear you without using your pain against you. People who respect confidentiality. People who tell you the truth without humiliating you. People who encourage responsibility, not excuses.

A strong brother does not simply say, "Whatever you do is fine." He reminds you who you said you wanted to be.

Professional help can be part of strength too. There are weights that require trained support. Seeking that support does not reduce your manhood. It protects your life and the people connected to it.

Carry the Assignment, Not Every Burden

Some men are carrying things that are not theirs.

Everybody's emergency. Everybody's expectations. Everybody's opinion. Everybody's consequences.

Leadership does not mean becoming the container for every problem around you.

Your assignment has weight, but it also has boundaries. Learn what belongs to you and what does not.

Ask: What responsibility is actually mine? What am I carrying because I am afraid to disappoint people? What burden belongs to another adult who needs to carry his or her own consequences? What weight can I set down without abandoning my values?

Heavy does not mean weak. But unnecessary weight can still break a strong man.

Feel the weight. Name the weight. Carry what is yours with discipline. Set down what was never assigned to you.

LEGACY WORK 7

Do not rush this page. Write what is true.

1. What weight am I carrying right now?

2. What part of it is actually mine?

3. What part can I set down?

4. Who can be a trustworthy spotter for me?

5. What recovery practice have I neglected?

THIS WEEK'S ACTION

Tell one trustworthy person what you are carrying instead of saying you are fine.

NOTES

CHAPTER 8

BROKEN MEN STILL BUILD

You do not have to be perfect to become useful.

Stop Waiting to Become Flawless

A lot of men are waiting to become perfect before they begin.

Once I heal everything. Once I stop doubting. Once I make enough money. Once my past stops bothering me. Once I feel completely ready.

That day may never come.

Growth does not usually happen before the work. A lot of growth happens because of the work. You become disciplined by practicing discipline. You become a better father by fathering with intention. You become a stronger communicator by having hard conversations with more skill than you had last time.

Your unfinished places do not automatically disqualify you.

They do require humility. They require accountability. They require you to know where you still need help. But you do not have to wait until every scar disappears before you build something meaningful.

Broken Is Not the Same as Harmful

There is an important distinction here. Being wounded does not give you permission to wound other people.

A man can be healing and still be responsible. He can admit where he is broken and still make sure his brokenness does not become somebody else's daily danger.

If your behavior is destructive, abusive, violent, addictive, or unsafe, building must include getting help and stopping the harm. Calling yourself "a work in progress" cannot become an excuse for repeatedly injuring people.

True growth becomes visible in changed behavior.

You do not have to be flawless. You do have to be accountable.

Build With What You Have

Maybe you do not have the resources you want yet. Start with what you have.

You have time somewhere. You have a phone. You have a notebook. You have one conversation you can make right. You have one habit you can change. You have one child who can receive more of your attention. You have one room you can bring more peace into.

Legacy often begins smaller than ego wants.

A man imagines a foundation, a company, a movement, a book, or generational wealth. Those things may come. But the first brick might be keeping your word this week.

Do not despise small construction.

A stable life is built the same way a wall is built. One aligned piece at a time.

Your Scar Can Become Instruction

A scar is not proof that the injury was good. It is proof that healing happened.

Some of the most useful wisdom you will ever give somebody will come from the places where you once struggled. Not because pain made you special, but because experience made certain lessons real.

The man who learned to control his temper can teach a younger man what reaction costs. The father who repaired a relationship can teach another father how to apologize. The man who rebuilt financially can explain patience better than somebody who never lost anything.

Do not romanticize pain. Use what you learned.

Your past becomes legacy when wisdom is extracted from it and lived forward.

Build While Becoming

You are allowed to build and become at the same time.

Write the book while improving your craft. Start the business while learning leadership. Repair the relationship while becoming more emotionally mature. Lead the prayer while deepening your faith. Show up to counseling while still feeling uncertain.

The goal is not to pretend you are finished. The goal is to keep moving in truth.

Your family does not need a flawless man. They need a man whose direction is trustworthy.

A man who can say, "I am still learning, but I am not hiding. I am still growing, but I am not quitting. I still have work to do, and I am doing it."

Broken men still build. Responsible men make sure the building process also includes repair.

LEGACY WORK 8

Do not rush this page. Write what is true.

1. What am I delaying until I feel completely ready?

2. What can I begin with what I already have?

3. Where do I need help before I keep building?

4. What past mistake contains a lesson I can use?

5. What would responsible progress look like this month?

THIS WEEK'S ACTION

Take the smallest real step toward the thing you keep postponing.

NOTES

CHAPTER 9

WHERE KINGS LAY THEIR ARMOR

Strength needs somewhere to recover.

The Danger of Permanent Armor

Armor has a purpose. It protects you in battle. The problem begins when a man forgets how to take it off.

Some men live in permanent fight mode. Always alert. Always producing. Always prepared for something to go wrong. They know how to be useful but not how to be still. They know how to protect everybody else but not how to receive care.

That kind of strength can become dangerous. Not because strength is bad, but because anything held too long becomes heavy.

If you never set the armor down, eventually the thing that protected you starts crushing you.

Rest Is Not Laziness

A lot of men have tied their value to output. If they are not working, fixing, providing, or producing, they feel guilty.

Rest then feels like irresponsibility.

But recovery is part of responsibility.

Your body needs sleep. Your mind needs quiet. Your spirit needs space where you are not performing. Your relationships need moments that are not organized around solving problems.

Rest is not the opposite of discipline. Healthy rest is one of discipline's responsibilities.

A tired man is more reactive. More impulsive. More likely to misread a situation. More likely to reach for shortcuts. Protecting rest protects judgment.

Find a Place Where You Can Be Known

Every man needs at least one place where he does not have to pretend.

Maybe it is a brother who knows more than your accomplishments. Maybe it is a therapist or counselor. Maybe it is prayer early in the morning. Maybe it is a trusted pastor, mentor, support group, or quiet journal.

The point is not the location. The point is truth.

Where can you say, "I am tired," without somebody using it to question your manhood? Where can you admit fear without being mocked? Where can you talk about temptation before temptation becomes consequence?

If you do not have that place, building one should become part of your legacy plan.

Let the People Who Love You Love You

Some men are comfortable giving love and uncomfortable receiving it.

We know how to provide. We know how to rescue. We know how to show up when somebody else is in trouble. But when somebody asks what we need, we say, "I'm good."

Sometimes "I'm good" is true. Sometimes it is armor.

Receiving care requires trust. It requires you to believe you can be valued even when you are not performing.

Allow safe people to support you. Let somebody cook for you, pray for you, listen to you, encourage you, or tell you to rest. Strength that cannot receive anything eventually becomes isolation.

Maintenance Is Part of the Mission

You maintain what you want to last.

Cars need maintenance. Houses need maintenance. Businesses need maintenance. Bodies, minds, marriages, friendships, and faith do too.

Do not wait until something breaks before you pay attention.

Schedule recovery before burnout. Have conversations before resentment. Ask for help before crisis. Take care of your body before pain forces you to.

You are not less of a man because you need maintenance. You are a wiser man when you stop treating yourself as disposable.

Your strength is not only in how much you can carry. It is in knowing when to lay the armor down so you can carry tomorrow well.

LEGACY WORK 9

Do not rush this page. Write what is true.

1. Where do I currently lay my armor?

2. Do I know how to rest without guilt?

3. What does exhaustion make me more likely to do?

4. Who knows the real version of me?

5. What kind of maintenance does my life need right now?

THIS WEEK'S ACTION

Protect one block of recovery time this week and treat it as a responsibility, not a reward.

NOTES

CHAPTER 10

THE BLOODLINE PRAYER

Live like your life is answering something older than you.

Somebody Wanted Better

Long before you knew what you were becoming, somebody in your family probably wanted better.

Maybe it was a grandmother praying over names. Maybe it was a father who made mistakes but still hoped his son would go further. Maybe it was a mother working two jobs and quietly believing her children would have more choices. Maybe it was an ancestor who never saw freedom the way you experience it but still survived long enough for your line to continue.

You are connected to prayers, sacrifices, mistakes, endurance, and hope that started before you.

That does not mean everything that happened in your bloodline was good. It means you have the power to decide what gets honored, what gets healed, and what gets ended.

Prayer as Participation

Prayer is not an excuse to avoid action.

If you pray for your family to become healthier, participate in that prayer by communicating differently. If you pray for financial stability, build habits that support it. If you pray for peace, stop feeding the chaos you keep asking God to remove.

Faith and responsibility belong in the same room.

A bloodline prayer becomes powerful when it turns into daily behavior.

You can pray with your mouth and contradict the prayer with your habits. Or you can let your choices become part of the answer.

Pray Forward

Most people pray about what they need now. Legacy asks you to pray forward.

Pray for the children you have and the grandchildren you may never meet. Pray for their character, not only their comfort. Pray that they know how to handle money without worshiping it. Pray that they know how to love without losing themselves. Pray that they can express emotion without being controlled by it.

Then ask what kind of example would make those prayers easier for them to live.

If you want your sons to be disciplined, let them see discipline. If you want your daughters to expect respect, let them see respect. If you want the next generation to value faith, let them see faith become practice.

Prayer forward. Live forward.

A Different Kind of Inheritance

Money matters. Property matters. Education matters. Opportunity matters.

But your children will inherit more than assets.

They will inherit your relationship with conflict. Your language around money. Your way of treating women. Your habits around work. Your response to stress. Your ability or inability to apologize. Your beliefs about God, family, and responsibility.

That inheritance begins while you are alive.

You are writing it in ordinary moments.

The question is not only, "What will I leave?" It is, "What are they already receiving from me?

Become the Prayer

There is something powerful about realizing you may already be living in an answer somebody asked God for.

You survived things that could have ended your story. You learned things nobody taught you. You are trying to build what you did not inherit.

Do not waste that opportunity by living carelessly.

Ask God for the strength to break what should not continue. Ask for wisdom to build what has never existed in your family. Ask for humility when success comes. Ask for endurance when the work feels slow.

Then get up and participate.

Let your name carry honor because your choices carry integrity. Let your life become the bridge between what was broken and what can be blessed.

LEGACY WORK 10

Do not rush this page. Write what is true.

1. What did the people before me survive so I could have more options?

2. What pattern should not continue through me?

3. What prayer for my family requires action from me?

4. What inheritance am I already giving through my habits?

5. What do I want the next generation to thank God for?

THIS WEEK'S ACTION

Write a short prayer for the generation after you and one action that agrees with that prayer.

NOTES

CHAPTER II

THE FINAL TEST OF A MAN

Character is what remains when nobody is watching.

The Private Test

Every man is tested more than once.

Some tests are public. A job loss. A breakup. A financial setback. A health scare. Everybody can see the pressure.

The deeper tests are often private.

What do you do when you know you could get away with something? What do you do when nobody would know you lied? What do you do when an attractive shortcut appears and your values are the only thing standing in the way?

Character is built where applause cannot reach.

A man can look disciplined in public and still be reckless in private. Legacy eventually reveals the difference.

Your Word Is a Contract With Yourself

Every time you keep a promise to yourself, you strengthen trust inside yourself.

Every time you repeatedly break your own word, something weakens.

You say you will stop. Then you do it again. You say you will show up. Then you disappear. You say family matters. Then they keep receiving your leftovers.

The issue is bigger than one missed promise. Your identity starts listening.

A tempered man becomes careful with his word. He does not promise everything. He commits more slowly because he intends to follow through.

Reliability is a form of power.

Faithfulness in Small Things

A lot of people want a big assignment. The question is whether you can be faithful in small responsibilities.

Can you return the call? Pay the bill? Keep the appointment? Finish the task? Tell the truth when a lie would be easier? Be kind to the person who cannot advance your career?

Legacy is built from small acts repeated long enough that they become character.

The man who waits for a dramatic moment to prove himself misses hundreds of quiet tests every week.

What Do You Guard?

The final test is not only about what you gain. It is about what you protect.

Your character. Your peace. Your family. Your name. Your faith. Your health. Your word.

Success can test a man just as much as failure. When money increases, does humility survive? When attention increases, does loyalty survive? When power increases, does integrity survive?

A legacy worth leaving is not simply a record of accomplishment. It is evidence that what mattered most was still intact when accomplishment arrived.

Pass the Test Again Tomorrow

There is no graduation from character.

You pass today's test and tomorrow brings another one.

That may sound exhausting, but it can also be freeing. You do not have to prove your whole life today. You only have to meet the next decision with the man you said you wanted to be.

When nobody is watching, keep your word.

When you are lonely, keep your standards.

When progress is slow, keep building.

When you fail, tell the truth, repair what you can, learn, and return.

The goal is not a perfect record. It is a trustworthy direction.

May they be able to say that you were a man of your word, a builder, a protector, and proof that change can become a way of life.

LEGACY WORK II

Do not rush this page. Write what is true.

1. Who am I when nobody is watching?

2. Where have I been breaking my own word?

3. What small responsibility keeps testing my character?

4. What am I protecting as I pursue success?

5. What would integrity require from me today?

THIS WEEK'S ACTION

Keep one promise to yourself for the next seven days with no negotiation.

NOTES

CHAPTER 12

THE FATHER YOU BECOME

Fatherhood is presence repeated over time.

Fatherhood Is More Than Biology

Fatherhood is not only a title. It is a responsibility to nurture, protect, teach, correct, guide, and remain present.

Some men become biological fathers. Some become stepfathers, mentors, coaches, uncles, teachers, leaders, or trusted men whose presence helps shape younger lives.

You father what you consistently protect and develop.

That means fatherhood begins with who you are becoming, because children learn as much from what you embody as from what you explain.

Become What You Needed

Many men enter fatherhood while still carrying questions about their own fathers.

Some fathers left. Some stayed but were emotionally distant. Some provided but did not know how to connect. Some were loving but inconsistent. Some caused real harm.

You cannot change the father you had. You can decide what kind of fatherhood moves through you.

You can become the man who listens. The man who apologizes. The man who says, "I love you," without waiting for a special occasion. The man who sets boundaries without humiliating. The man whose children know correction and connection can exist together.

Becoming what you needed does not erase what you missed. It gives the absence a different ending.

Presence Over Performance

Children do not need an impressive father as much as they need an available one.

They need your eyes when they are talking. Your attention when they are scared. Your questions when they are confused. Your stability when their emotions are larger than their vocabulary.

Presence is not perfection. You will miss things. You will get tired. You will answer badly sometimes.

The important part is repair.

A father who can say, "I was wrong. I should not have spoken to you that way," teaches accountability without giving a lecture about accountability.

Teach What You Want Repeated

Every household has a curriculum whether it is written or not.

Children are learning how adults handle money, anger, disappointment, affection, conflict, work, faith, rest, and responsibility.

Ask yourself what your home is teaching.

If you want your children to communicate, let them see communication. If you want them to value health, let them see you care for your body. If you want them to respect women, let them watch how you speak to and about women. If you want them to own mistakes, let them see you own yours.

Your behavior is the textbook they read every day.

Father the Future

A focused father changes generations.

Not because he controls everything, but because he creates a reliable point of reference.

Your children will make their own choices. Your job is not to manufacture them into copies of you. Your job is to give them love, truth, structure, faith, safety, responsibility, and enough room to become themselves.

One day somebody may ask where the shift in your family began.

Let your name come up not because you were perfect, but because you were present. Because you faced what earlier generations avoided. Because you chose to raise the future instead of only reacting to the past.

LEGACY WORK 12

Do not rush this page. Write what is true.

1. What did I need from a father that I can now give?

2. How do the younger people around me experience my presence?

3. What do my children learn from the way I handle mistakes?

4. Where do I need to apologize or reconnect?

5. What value do I want my household to practice, not just discuss?

THIS WEEK'S ACTION

Create one simple family practice that reflects a value you want repeated.

NOTES

NOTES

CHAPTER 14

LEGACY IS WRITTEN IN ACTION

Your intentions matter. Your repetitions matter more.

Legacy Is Happening Now

Words fade. Money gets spent. Looks change. Titles eventually belong to somebody else.

What remains is impact.

Legacy is not only what people say at your funeral. It is what your choices have already placed inside other people.

It is in the way your daughter learns what respect feels like. It is in the way your son handles pressure. It is in the confidence of somebody you mentored. It is in the stability of a family system you helped create.

Legacy is happening while you are alive.

Intention Is Not Execution

Most men have good intentions.

They intend to be more patient. Intend to save money. Intend to spend more time with family. Intend to repair the relationship. Intend to pray more. Intend to change a habit.

Intentions matter because they reveal desire. But desire without execution does not become legacy.

Your life is shaped by what you repeatedly do.

The quiet decisions matter. Holding your tongue when anger wants the last word. Going home when temptation offers another option. Keeping the appointment. Telling the truth. Showing up for the game, recital, dinner, conversation, or ordinary Tuesday night.

Legacy is written in small ink before anybody reads the final page.

Build Systems That Outlive Motivation

If something matters, give it structure.

Family time belongs on the calendar. Saving belongs in an automatic system. Health belongs in a routine. Faith belongs in practice. Relationships need scheduled attention. Important documents need organization. Values need traditions.

Systems turn belief into behavior.

Do not make the next generation guess what mattered to you. Put your values into repeatable practices.

Maybe every Sunday the family eats together. Maybe every year you review financial goals. Maybe birthdays include a written letter. Maybe sons and daughters know they can ask hard questions without being punished for asking.

Traditions are values given a schedule.

Imagine the Grandchild You May Never Meet

Picture a grandson decades from now standing at a decision point.

He is angry. He has been disrespected. He has the opportunity to react or lead.

He chooses discipline.

Maybe he never met you. Maybe he only knows your name from stories. But something you started became normal in the family. Men learned to talk. Men learned to apologize. Men learned to pray. Men learned to keep their word. Men learned to choose responsibility over ego.

That is generational impact.

You may never witness the full result of what you build. Build it anyway.

The Charge

Do not finish this book and return to normal.

Finish what you start. Love with intention. Lead with honor. Forgive where forgiveness is possible without abandoning wisdom. Speak life. Pray without shame. Build even when tired. Rest before burnout. Ask for help before crisis. Show up when it is inconvenient.

Do not wait for a dramatic legacy moment. Use today.

Call your child. Fix the budget. Schedule the appointment. Write the letter. Have the conversation. Keep the promise. Start the savings account. Apologize. Set the boundary. Take the walk. Open the Bible. Sit in silence. Ask the question.

Legacy is not something you leave one day.

It is something you live today.

And the standard lives on through what you choose next.

LEGACY WORK 14

Do not rush this page. Write what is true.

1. If my current habits became family traditions, would I be proud?

2. What do my repeated actions say I value?

3. What system could make one important value easier to live?

4. What do I want a grandchild to know about my name?

5. What is the next action that would make my legacy more intentional?

THIS WEEK'S ACTION

Choose one legacy system to start now: savings, family time, letters, health, prayer, mentoring, or another repeatable practice.

NOTES

FINAL WORD

From Raymond Hendricks to You, the Reader

To my brother reading this,

You made it to the end of the book, but the real work begins after the last page.

Tempered Legacy was never meant to become another collection of ideas you agree with and forget. It was written to make you look at what is moving through you and what will move forward because of you.

You have looked at self government, purpose, inherited silence, old wounds, commitment, personal code, emotional weight, unfinished growth, rest, prayer, character, fatherhood, sons, and action.

Now the question is simple: what will you live?

You do not have to change everything today. You do need to choose something today.

Heal what you can. Repair what you damaged. Build what your family needs. Tell the truth. Pray. Rest. Lead. Learn. Repeat.

Your name carries weight because people will attach experiences to it. Let those experiences include honesty, safety, discipline, love, accountability, faith, and presence.

You are not required to become a perfect man. You are responsible for becoming a more intentional one.

May your children receive more peace because you did this work. May the men around you become more honest because you were willing to be honest. May the people who come after you inherit systems, language, faith, wisdom, and examples that make their road stronger.

The standard lives on when you live it.

Raymond Hendricks
Founder, Men of Tempered Strength

LEGACY AFFIRMATION

A Daily Declaration for Tempered Men

I am the answer to a bloodline prayer.

I am not what broke me. I am what I choose to build from here.

I carry strength with discipline, not pride.

I lead with truth, not performance.

I protect what matters without losing myself.

I own my mistakes and repair what I can.

I heal what should never be passed down.

I speak life into sons, wisdom into brothers, dignity into daughters, and honor into my name.

I do not need perfection to practice responsibility.

I can rest without quitting.

I can feel without surrendering control.

I can forgive without abandoning wisdom.

I can become the turning point.

I can become the example.

My legacy is not only what I leave.

My legacy is what I live.

REFLECTION QUESTIONS

1. What generational pattern am I committed to breaking now?

2. How will I measure my legacy beyond money, titles, or attention?

3. What five values will form my personal code?

4. Who in my life needs to hear 'I see you,' 'I love you,' or 'I was wrong' from me?

5. What part of my past still affects the way I lead today?

6. Where do I need more structure instead of more motivation?

7. What does my calendar reveal about what I truly value?

8. How do the people closest to me experience me under pressure?

9. What family practice or tradition do I want to begin?

10. Who can hold me accountable to the man I say I am becoming?

11. What am I carrying that I need help carrying?

12. Where do I need to repair trust through consistent behavior?

13. What am I building that should outlive me?

14. What action will I take in the next seven days to make my legacy more intentional?

THE LEGACY COMMITMENT

I accept responsibility for the man I am becoming and for the patterns I allow to move through me.

I will not use my past as permission to repeat harm.

I will tell myself the truth.

I will build discipline where I have depended on emotion.

I will protect the people I love with presence, honesty, boundaries, and consistency.

I will ask for help when the weight exceeds what I can carry alone.

I will repair what I can when I cause harm.

I will build systems that support the values I claim to hold.

I will live with faith and responsibility in the same room.

I will remember that my legacy is being written before I am gone.

I will live in a way that gives the next generation something stronger to stand on.

Signed: ____

Date:

____

14 DAY LEGACY PRACTICE

Two weeks of turning principle into practice

A legacy does not change because you finished a book. It changes when your daily decisions begin agreeing with the man you say you want to become.

Use the next fourteen days as a reset. Do one practice each day. Keep the action simple enough to complete and honest enough to matter. At the end of two weeks, do not ask whether you were perfect. Ask whether you became more intentional.

TODAY'S PRACTICE

Begin the day before the world gets your attention. Spend ten quiet minutes in prayer, reflection, or journaling. Write the one quality you want to lead with today.

REFLECTION

What tried to take control of my mood today, and how did I respond?

TODAY'S PRACTICE

Identify one place where you have been avoiding honesty with yourself. Write the truth in one sentence without blaming anybody else.

REFLECTION

What becomes possible now that I have named what is true?

TODAY'S PRACTICE

Choose one promise you can keep today. Make it small and measurable. Complete it even if your mood changes.

REFLECTION

How did keeping my word affect the way I saw myself?

TODAY'S PRACTICE

Tell a child, younger man, family member, or friend something strengthening that you wish someone had told you earlier.

REFLECTION

What did I say, and why did it matter?

TODAY'S PRACTICE

Make one repair. Apologize, return the call, correct the mistake, replace what you damaged, or take responsibility where you have been avoiding it.

REFLECTION

What did responsibility require from me today?

TODAY'S PRACTICE

Remove one unnecessary distraction for the day. Limit the app, decline the argument, turn off the noise, or create an hour without interruption.

REFLECTION

What did I notice when the noise became quieter?

TODAY'S PRACTICE

Look back at the first six days. Name one win, one pattern, and one adjustment you need to make.

REFLECTION

Where am I already becoming more intentional?

TODAY'S PRACTICE

Do one thing that supports your physical health: walk, train, stretch, hydrate, prepare a better meal, or get the sleep you have been avoiding.

REFLECTION

How does caring for my body strengthen the way I lead?

TODAY'S PRACTICE

Read your personal code. If you have not written one, write five standards today. Choose one standard to practice deliberately.

REFLECTION

Which standard was hardest to live today?

TODAY'S PRACTICE

Have one conversation you have been postponing. Do not go in to win. Go in to be clear, calm, and responsible.

REFLECTION

What did I learn by staying present instead of avoiding the conversation?

TODAY'S PRACTICE

Create thirty minutes where you are not producing for anybody. Rest, pray, walk, sit quietly, or talk to somebody safe.

REFLECTION

What did I feel once I stopped performing?

TODAY'S PRACTICE

Turn one value into a system. Put family time on the calendar, automate savings, schedule workouts, set a weekly check in, or create a recurring practice.

REFLECTION

What value did I give structure today?

TODAY'S PRACTICE

Write a prayer or statement of hope for the generation after you. Then write one behavior that agrees with that prayer.

REFLECTION

What future am I asking for, and how am I helping build it?

TODAY'S PRACTICE

Review the last two weeks. Choose three practices you will carry forward for the next ninety days. Write them as commitments, not wishes.

REFLECTION

What three actions will become part of the legacy I live from here?

ALSO BY RAYMOND HENDRICKS

TEMPERED MIND

The Choice Between Chaos and Clarity

TEMPERED STRENGTH

The Disciplined Man's Guide to Emotional Mastery, Legacy, and Real Growth

LEADERSHIP UNDER PRESSURE

6 Principles for Leading Yourself and Others

MANIFEST

Stop Wishing. Start Becoming.

ABOUT THE AUTHOR

Raymond Hendricks is an author, speaker, entrepreneur, and founder of Men of Tempered Strength, a movement centered on accountability, emotional discipline, resilience, leadership, and legacy.

Through his books, speaking, and programs, Raymond challenges people to move beyond temporary motivation and take greater ownership of how they respond, lead, rebuild, and grow.

His work is grounded in a simple belief: transformation requires participation.

To learn more about Raymond Hendricks, his books, speaking, and programs, visit rayhendricksspeaks.com.

www.ingramcontent.com/pod-product-compliance
Lightning Source LLC
LaVergne TN
LVHW100732061126
851857LV00011B/506